THE PHILLIP KEVEREN SERIES — PIANO SOLO

THE HYMN COLLECTION

CONTENTS

2 ALL HAIL THE POWER OF JESUS' NAME

4 BREATHE ON ME, BREATH OF GOD

6 COME, THOU ALMIGHTY KING

8 COME, THOU FOUNT OF EVERY BLESSING

12 CROWN HIM WITH MANY CROWNS

15 GOD THE OMNIPOTENT!

18 GOD WILL TAKE CARE OF YOU

24 I LOVE TO TELL THE STORY

21 I SURRENDER ALL

26 I'VE GOT PEACE LIKE A RIVER

29 IMMORTAL, INVISIBLE

32 O WORSHIP THE KING

36 PRAISE TO THE LORD, THE ALMIGHTY

38 SOFTLY AND TENDERLY

40 THIS IS MY FATHER'S WORLD

42 'TIS SO SWEET TO TRUST IN JESUS

45 WERE YOU THERE?

48 Hymn Texts

— PIANO LEVEL —
LATE INTERMEDIATE/EARLY ADVANCED

ISBN 978-0-634-06874-4

HAL•LEONARD®
CORPORATION

7777 W. BLEMOUND RD. P.O. BOX 13819 MILWAUKEE, WI 53213

In Australia Contact:
Hal Leonard Australia Pty. Ltd.
22 Taunton Drive   P.O. Box 5130
Cheltenham East, 3192 Victoria, Australia
Email: ausadmin@halleonard.com

Visit Hal Leonard Online at
www.halleonard.com
Visit Phillip at
www.PhillipKeveren.com

ALL HAIL THE POWER OF JESUS' NAME

Words by EDWARD PERRONET
Altered by JOHN RIPPON
Music by OLIVER HOLDEN
Arranged by Phillip Keveren

With jubilance

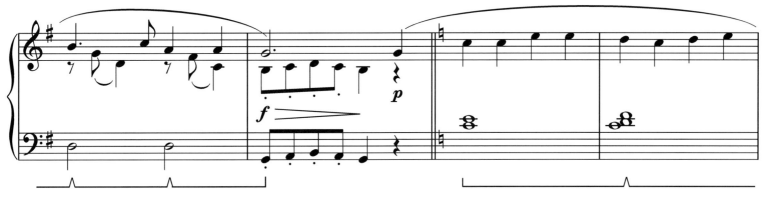

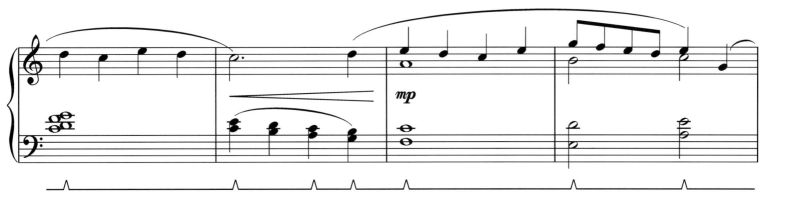

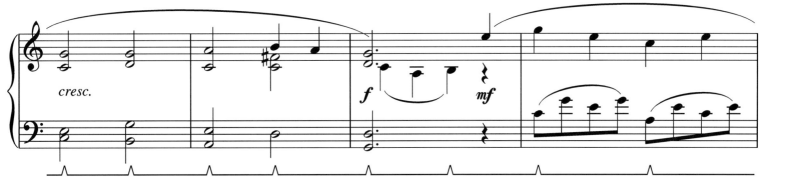

BREATHE ON ME, BREATH OF GOD

Words by EDWIN HATCH
Music by ROBERT JACKSON
Arranged by Phillip Keveren

Prayerfully

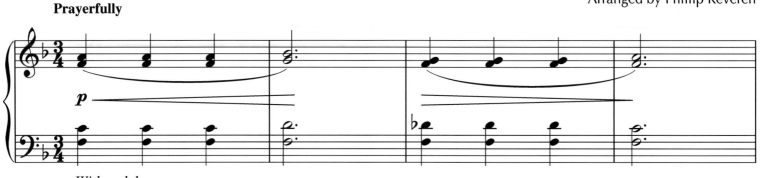

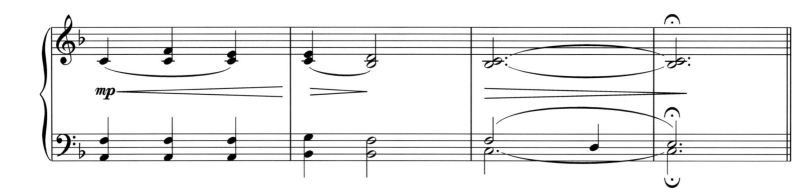

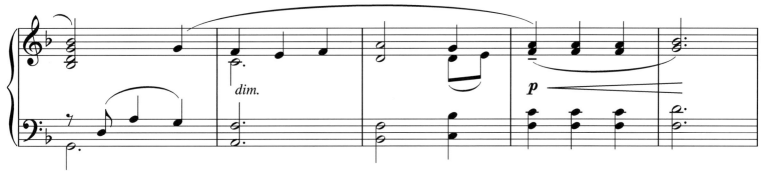

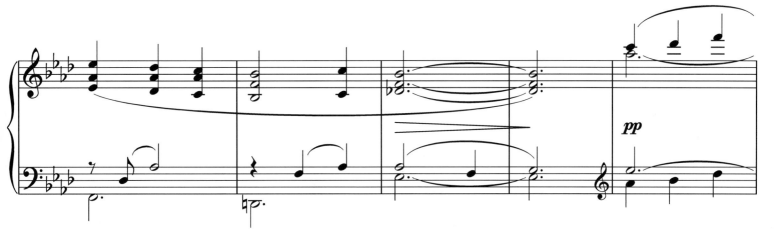

COME, THOU ALMIGHTY KING

Traditional
Music by FELICE DE GIARDINI
Arranged by Phillip Keveren

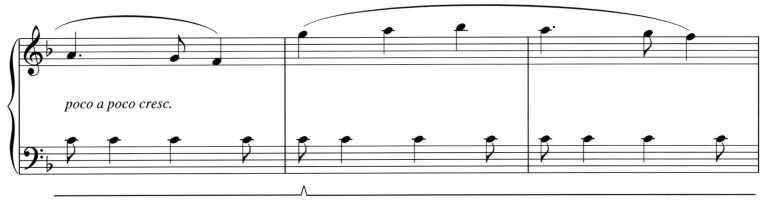

poco a poco cresc.

broaden

f

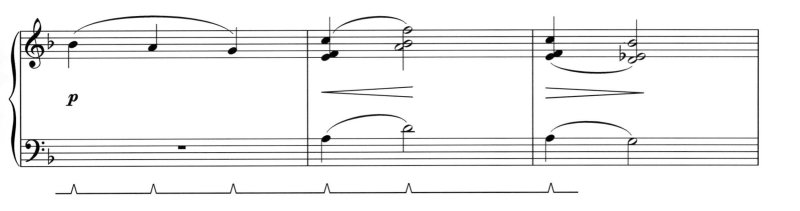

p

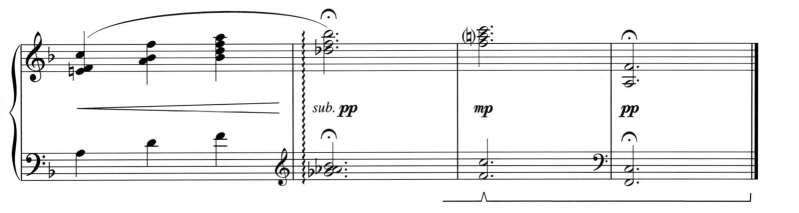

sub. *pp*

mp

pp

COME, THOU FOUNT OF EVERY BLESSING

Words by ROBERT ROBINSON
Music by *The Sacred Harp*
Arranged by Phillip Keveren

A rippling stream (♩. = 54)

pp

Ped. continuously

cresc.

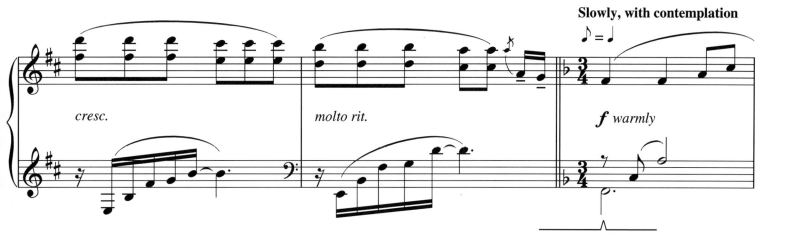

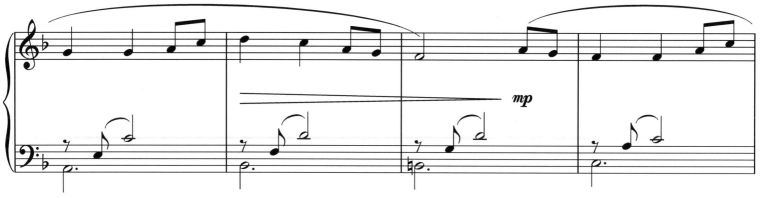

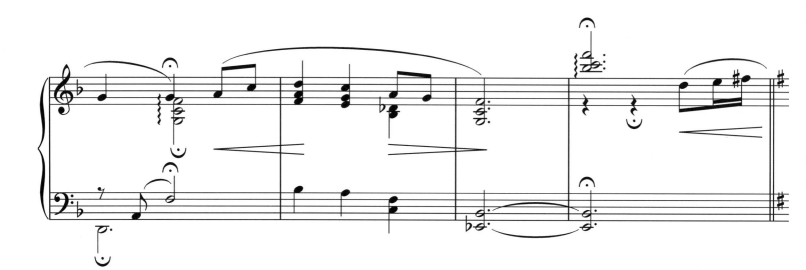

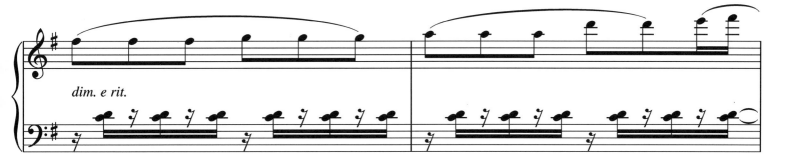

dim. e rit.

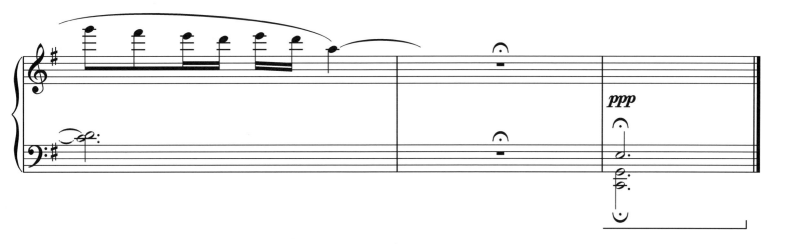

ppp

CROWN HIM WITH MANY CROWNS

Words by MATTHEW BRIDGES and GODFREY THRING
Music by GEORGE JOB ELVEY
Arranged by Phillip Keveren

With fanfare (♩ = 132)

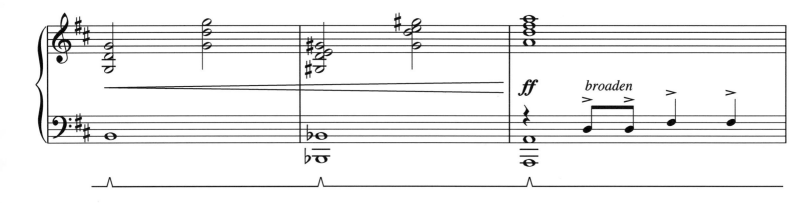

With dignity (♩ = 108)

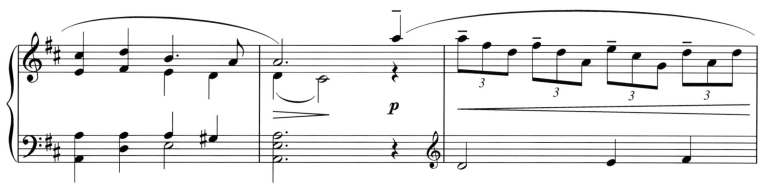

Brightly ($\quarternote$ = 156)

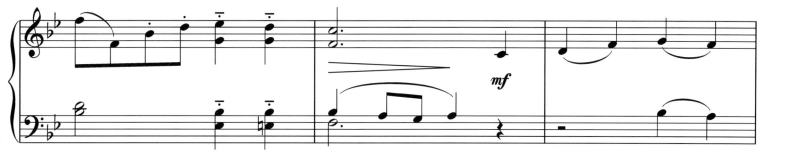

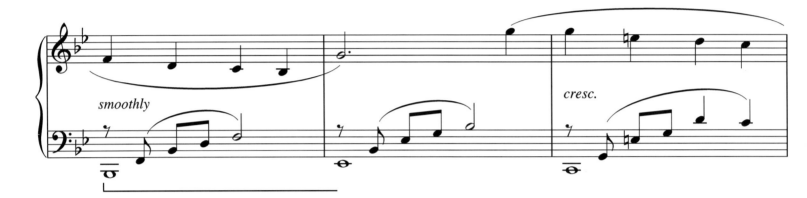

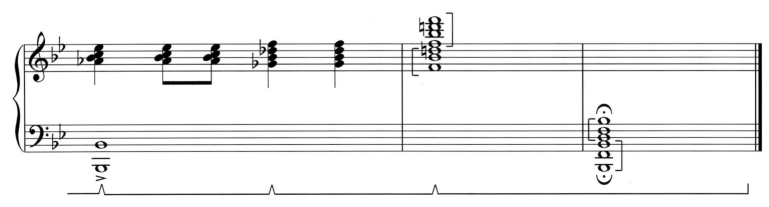

GOD THE OMNIPOTENT!

Words by HENRY F. CHORLEY and JOHN ELLERTON
Music by ALEXIS T. LVOV
Arranged by Phillip Keveren

Briskly (♩ = 132-138)

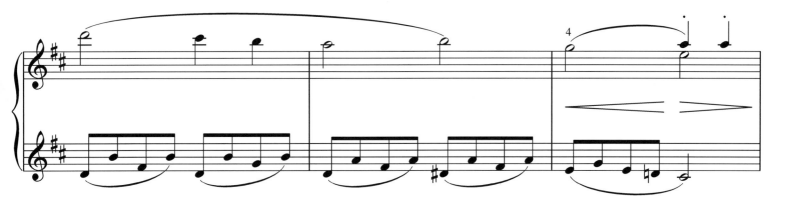

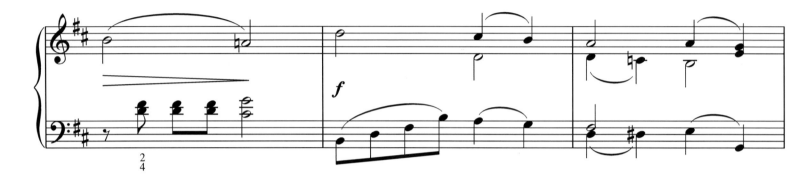

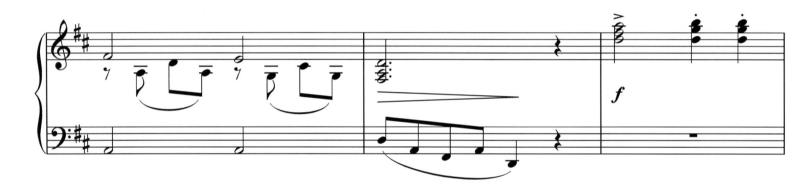

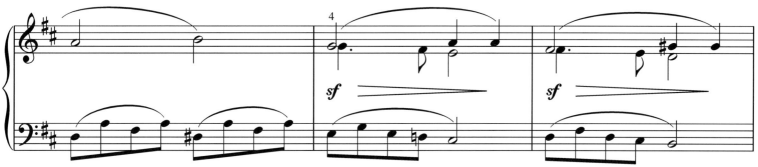

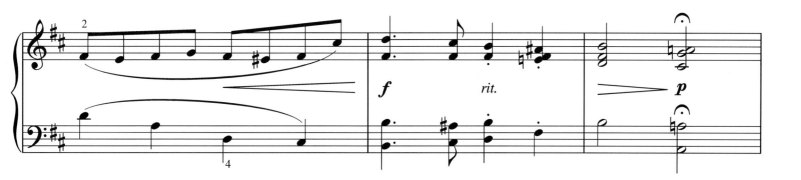

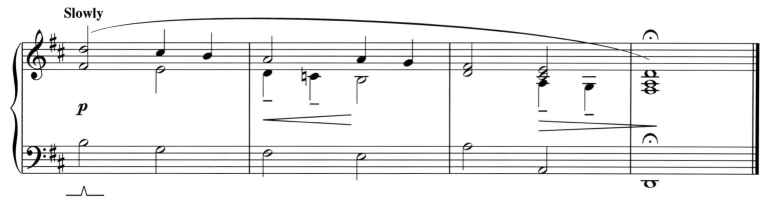

GOD WILL TAKE CARE OF YOU

Words by CIVILLA D. MARTIN
Music by STILLMAN MARTIN
Arranged by Phillip Keveren

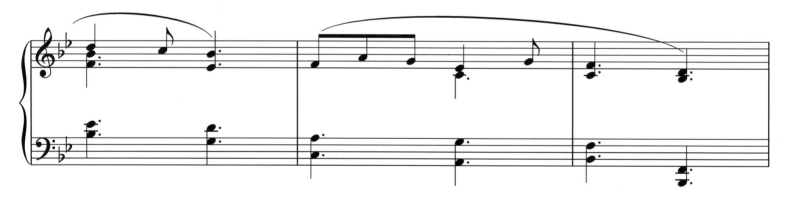

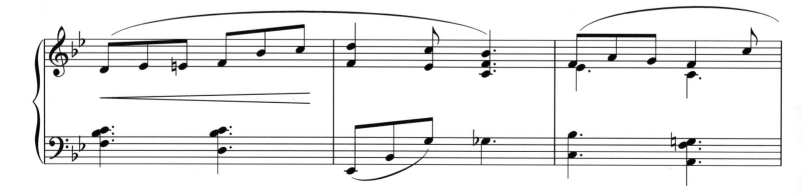

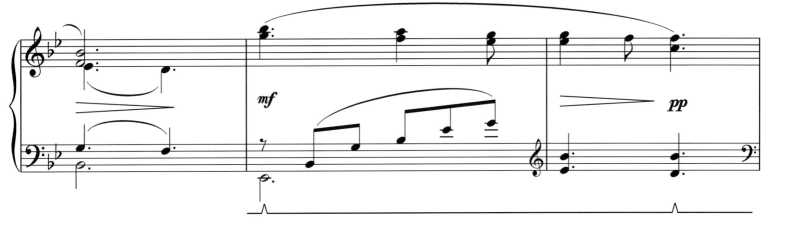

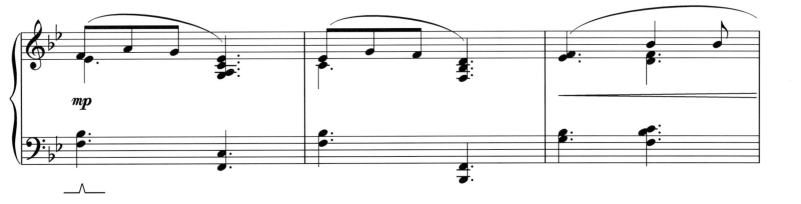

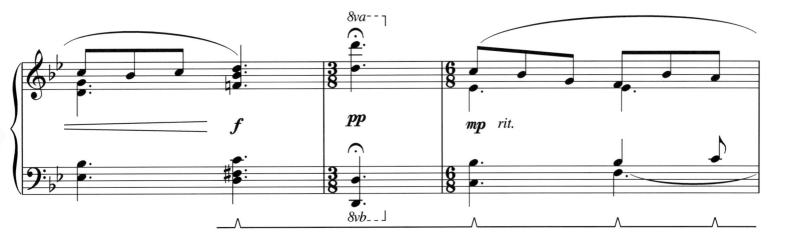

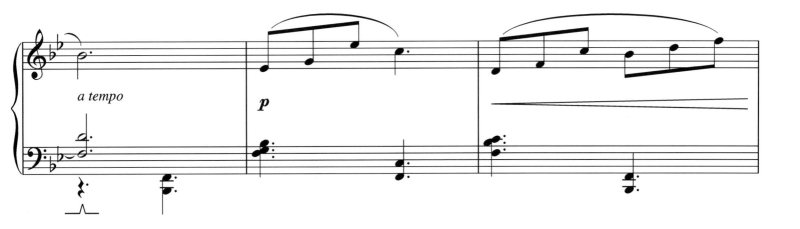

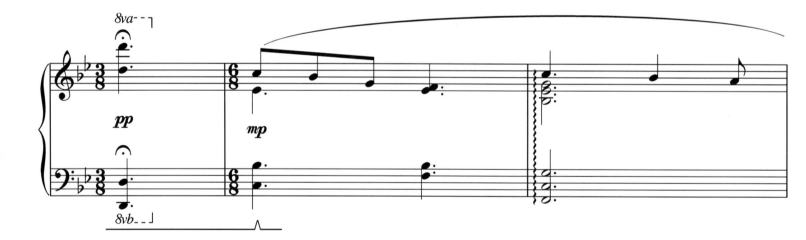

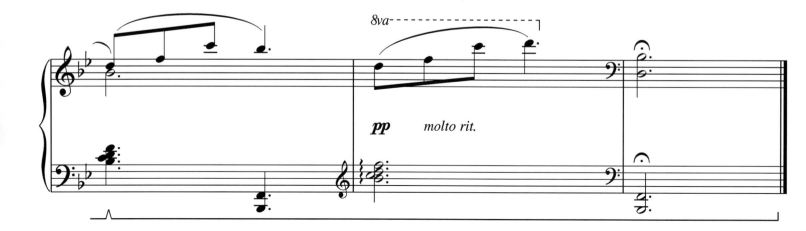

I SURRENDER ALL

Words by J.W. VAN DEVENTER
Music by W.S. WEEDEN
Arranged by Phillip Keveren

With deep conviction, freely

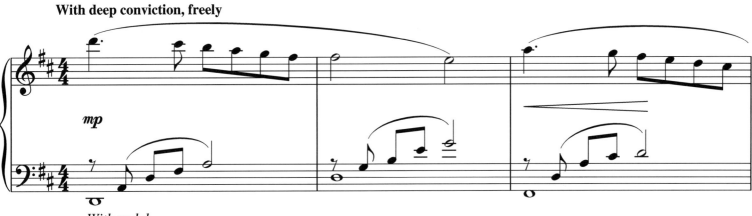

With pedal

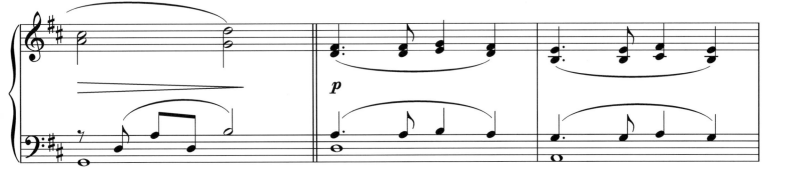

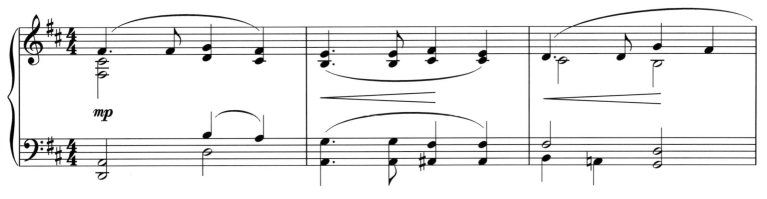

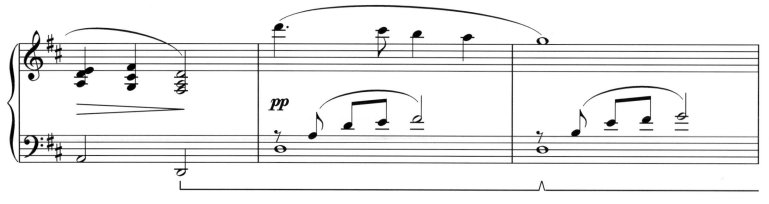

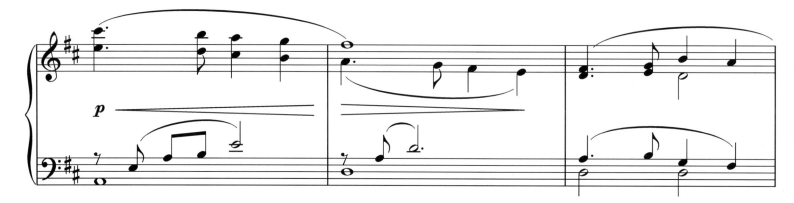

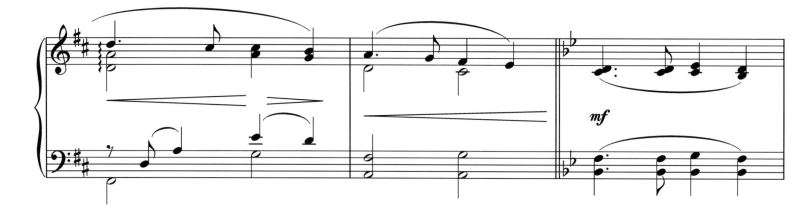

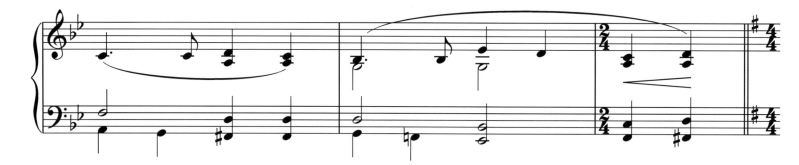

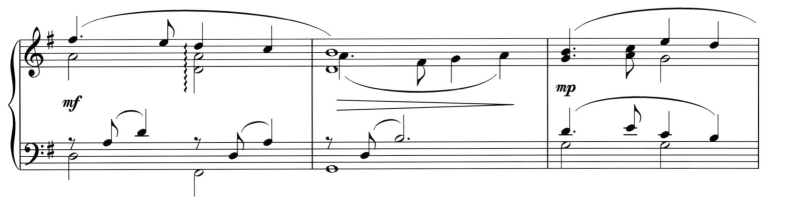

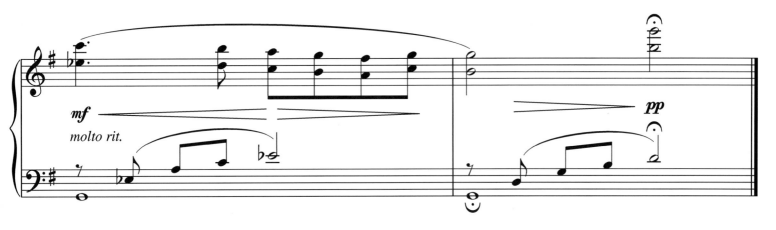

I LOVE TO TELL THE STORY

Words by A. CATHERINE HANKEY
Music by WILLIAM G. FISCHER
Arranged by Phillip Keveren

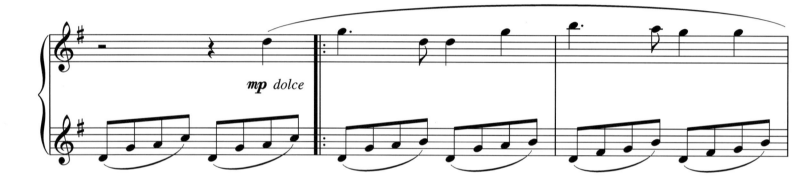

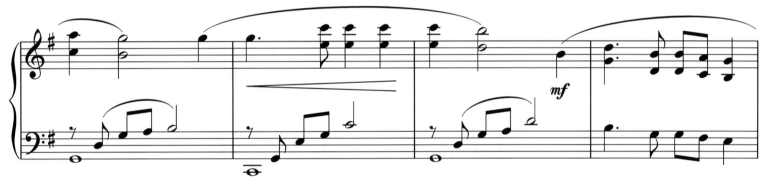

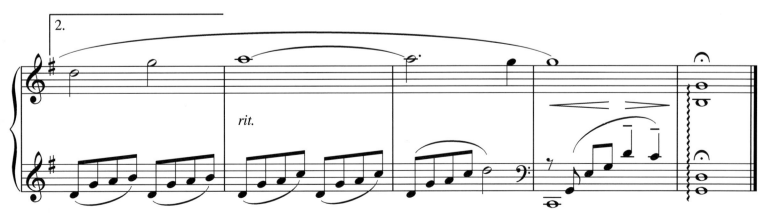

I'VE GOT PEACE LIKE A RIVER

Traditional
Arranged by Phillip Keveren

Gently flowing (♩ = 112)

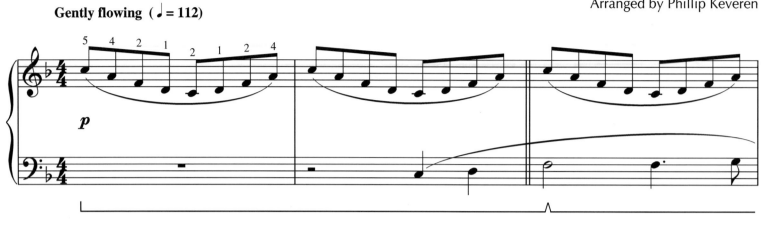

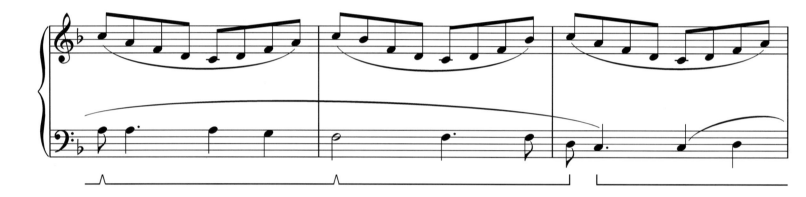

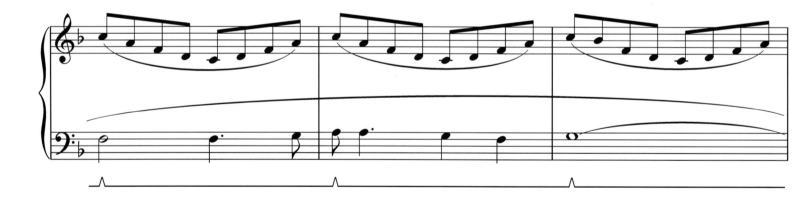

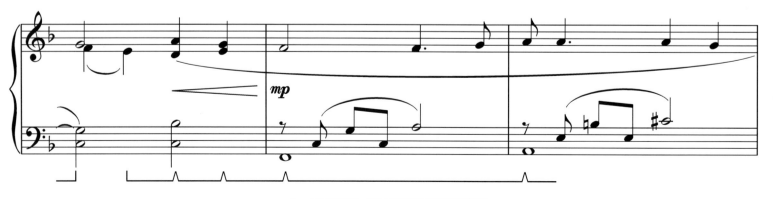

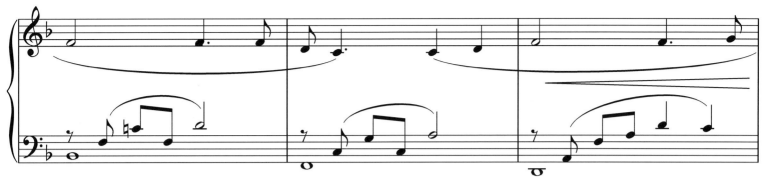

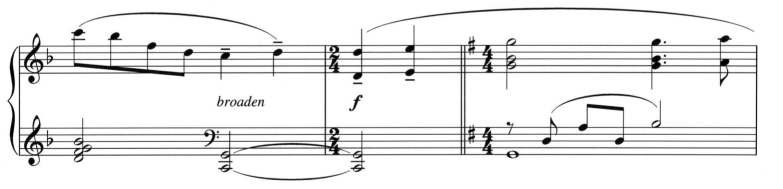

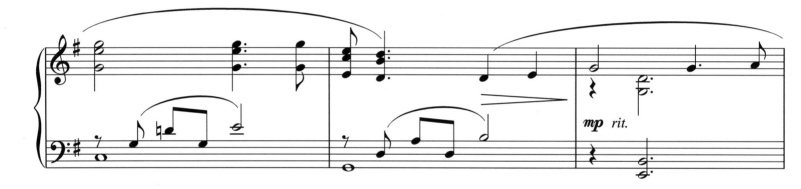

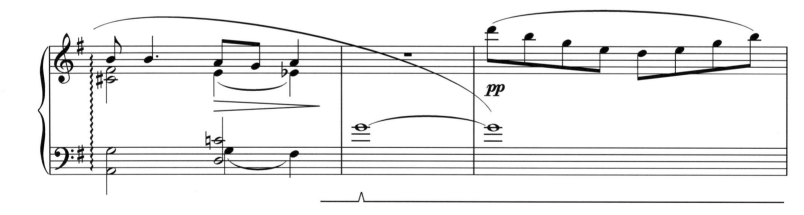

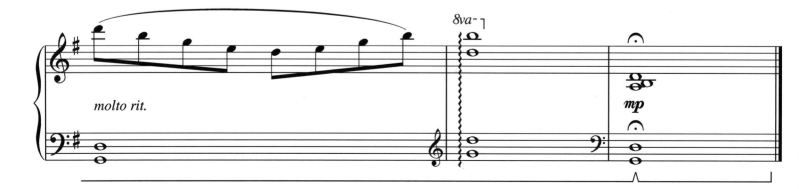

IMMORTAL, INVISIBLE

Words by WALTER CHALMERS SMITH
Traditional Welsh Melody
From JOHN ROBERTS' *Canaidau Y Cyssegr*
Arranged by Phillip Keveren

Passionately (♩ = 146-152)

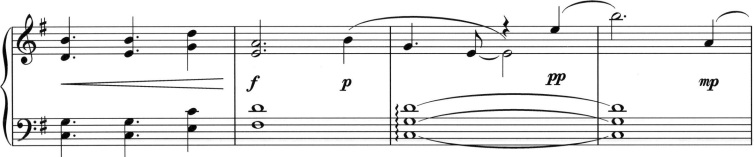

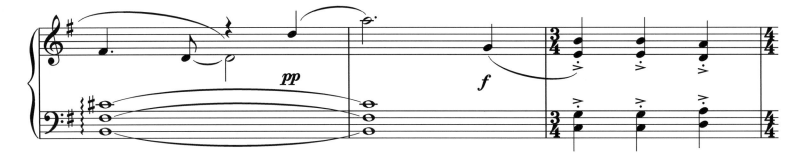

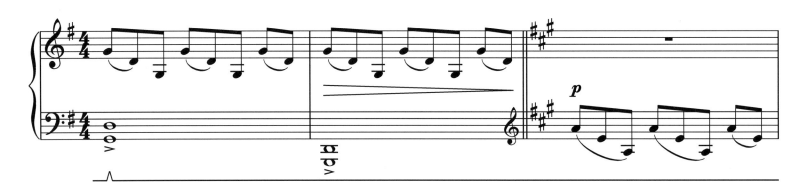

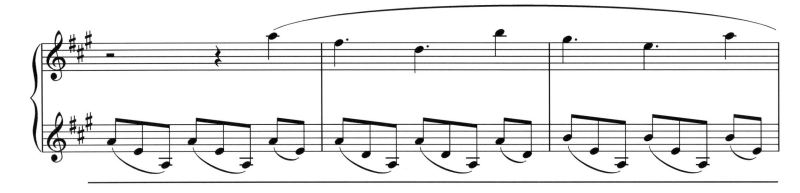

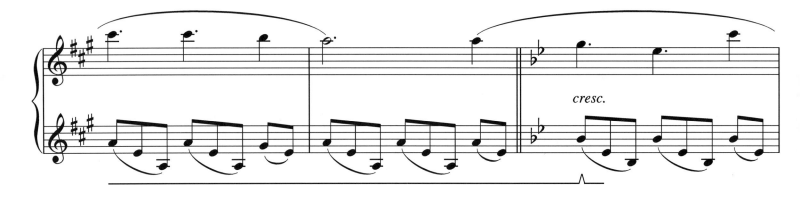

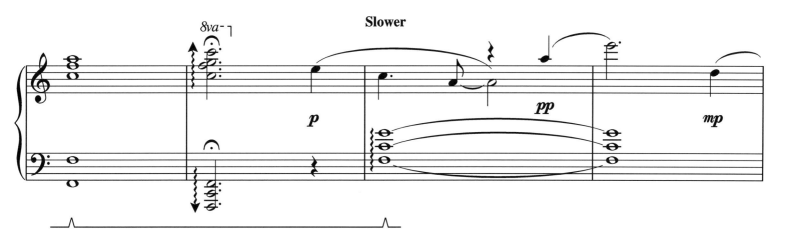

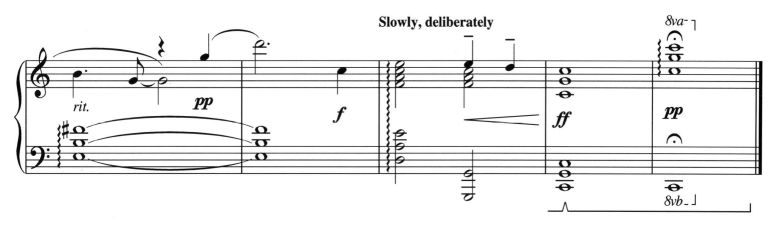

O WORSHIP THE KING

Words by ROBERT GRANT
Music attributed to JOHANN MICHAEL HAYDN
Arranged by Phillip Keveren

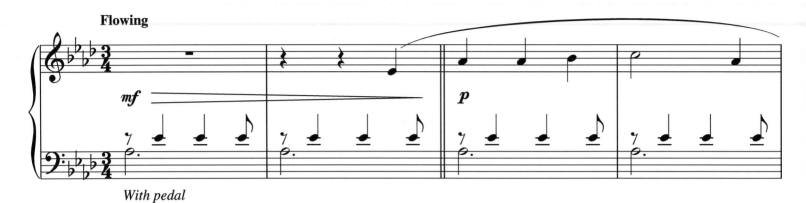

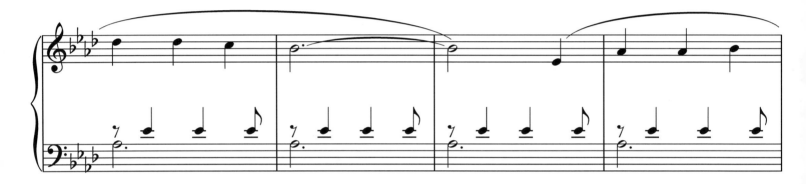

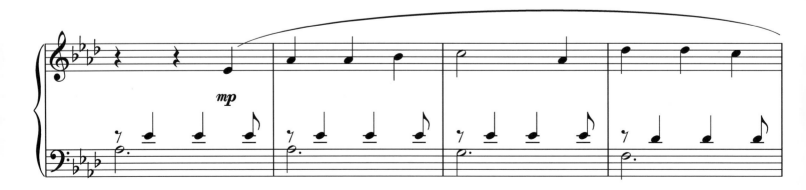

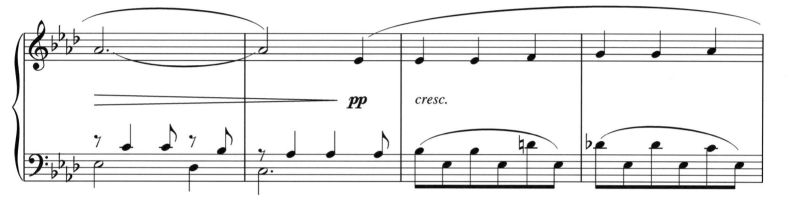

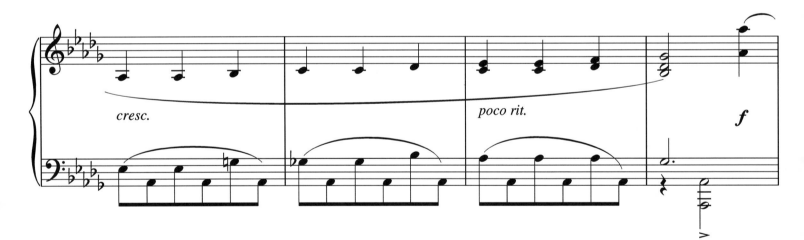

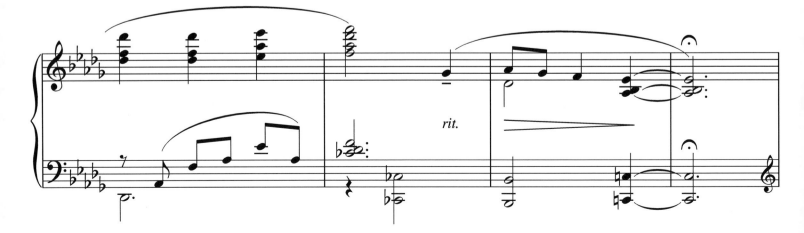

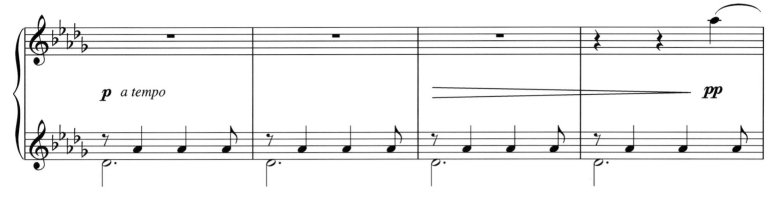

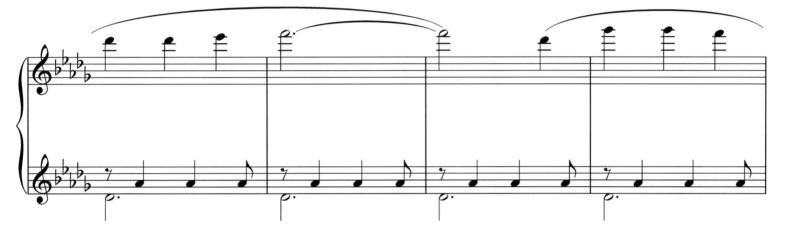

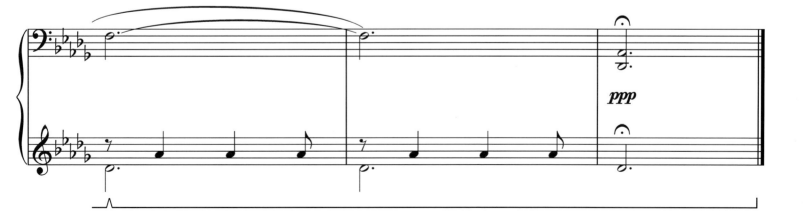

PRAISE TO THE LORD, THE ALMIGHTY

Words by JOACHIM NEANDER
Translated by CATHERINE WINKWORTH
Music from *Erneuerten Gesangbuch*
Arranged by Phillip Keveren

Spirited (♩ = 144)

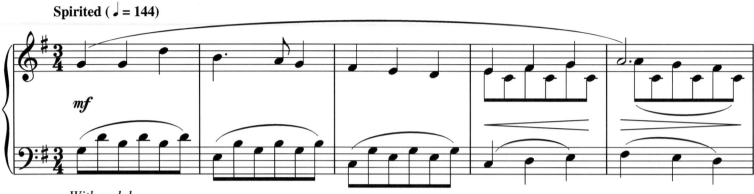

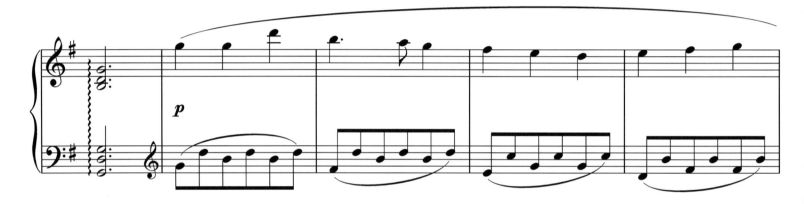

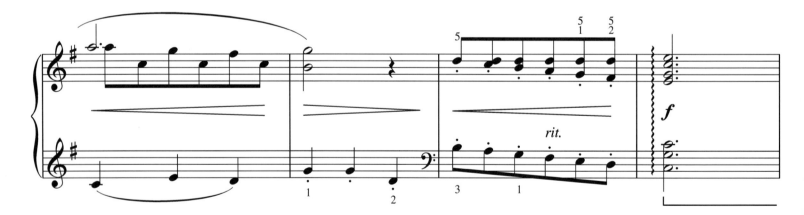

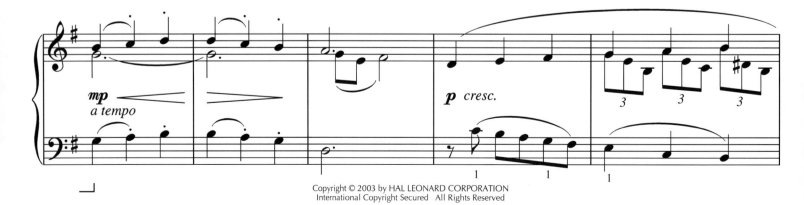

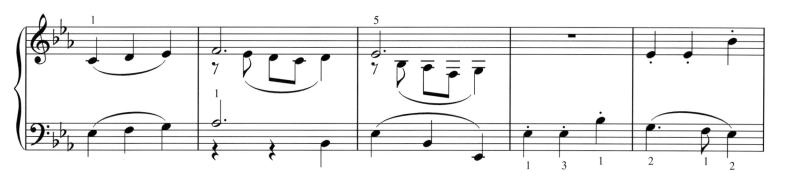

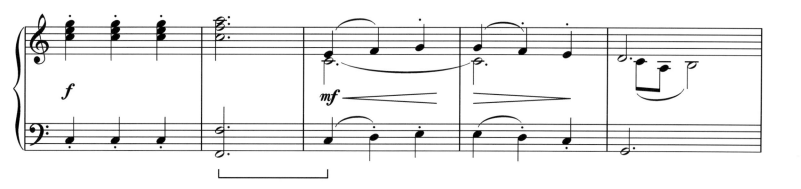

SOFTLY AND TENDERLY

Words and Music by WILL L. THOMPSON
Arranged by Phillip Keveren

Slowly, gently

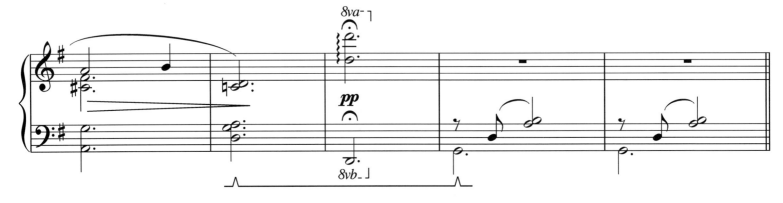

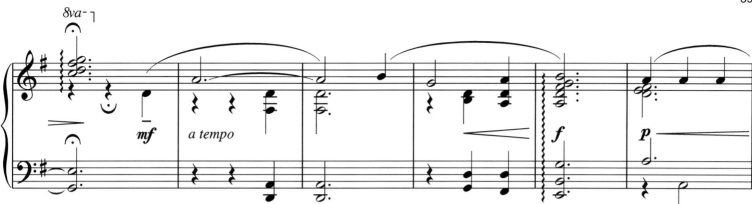

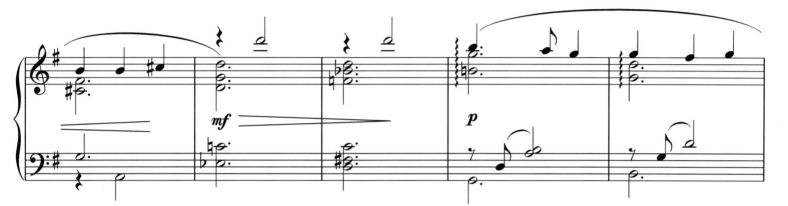

THIS IS MY FATHER'S WORLD

Words by MALTBIE D. BABCOCK
Music by FRANKLIN L. SHEPPARD
Arranged by Phillip Keveren

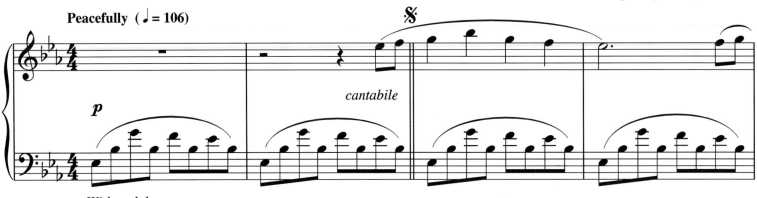

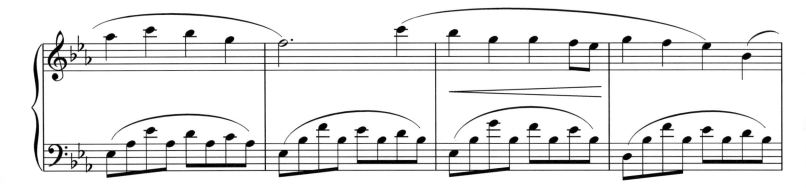

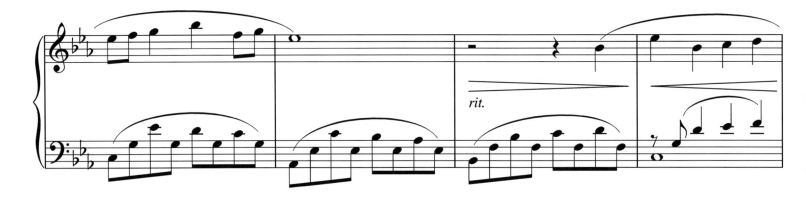

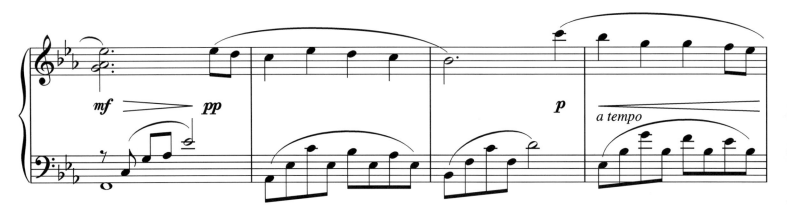

To Coda ⊕

Slightly slower

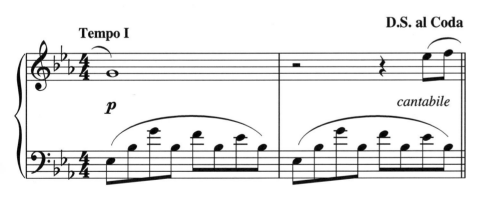

Tempo I

D.S. al Coda ⊕

CODA ⊕

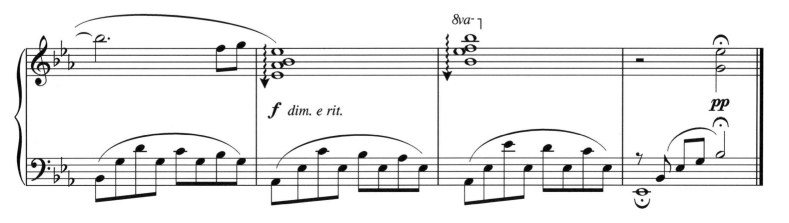

'TIS SO SWEET TO TRUST IN JESUS

Words by LOUISA M.R. STEAD
Music by WILLIAM J. KIRKPATRICK
Arranged by Phillip Keveren

Slowly, rubato

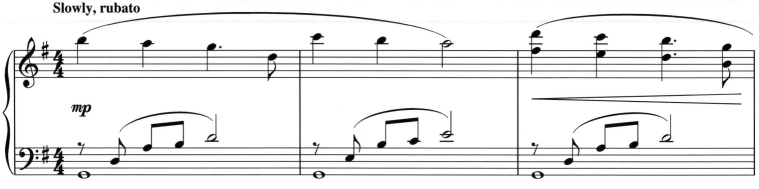

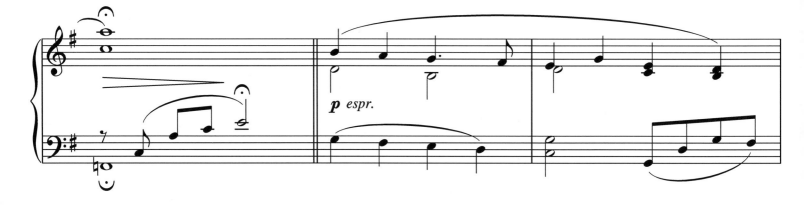

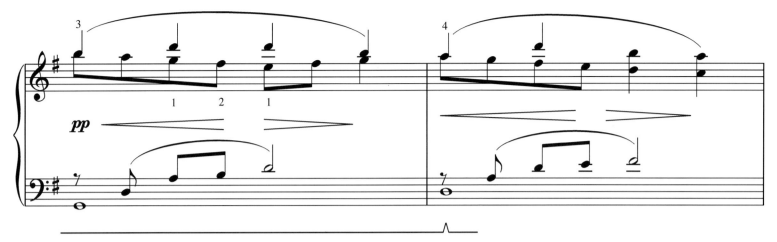

WERE YOU THERE?

Traditional Spiritual
Arranged by Phillip Keveren

Solemnly

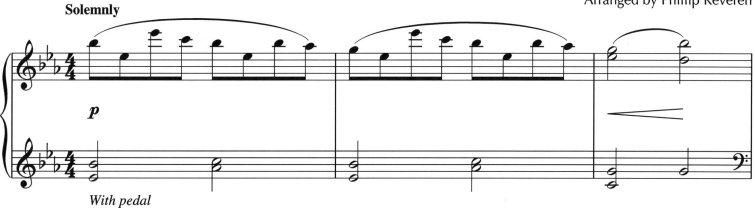

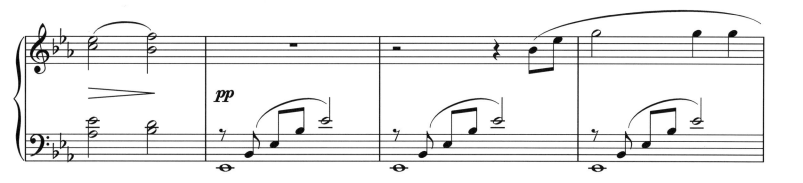

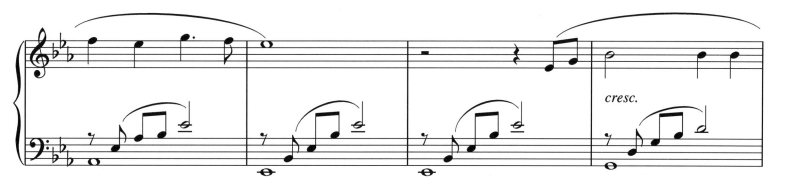

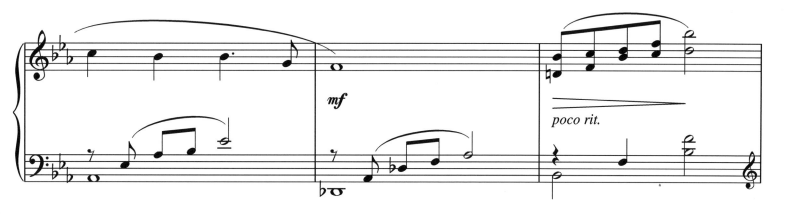

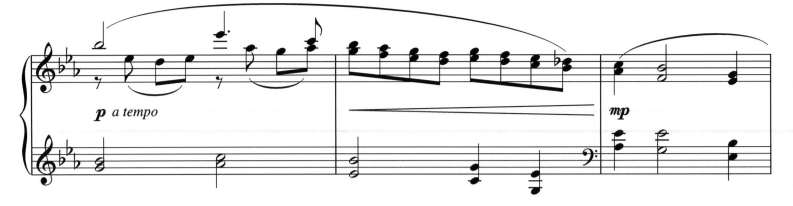

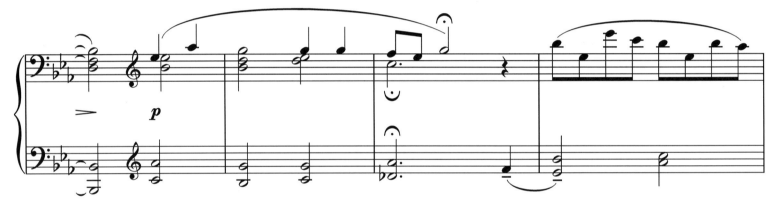

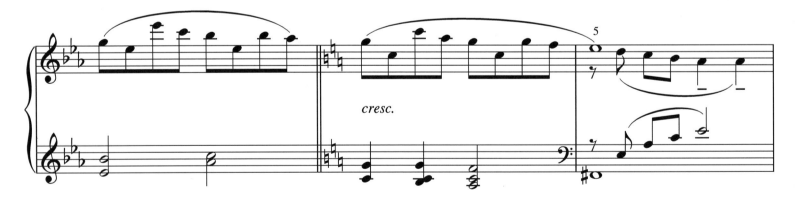

Più mosso

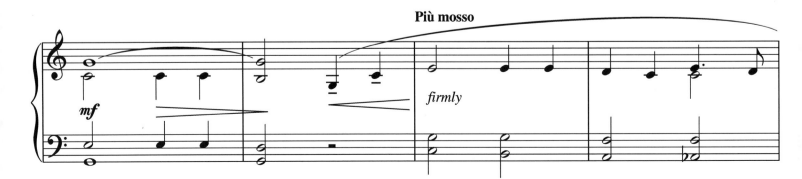

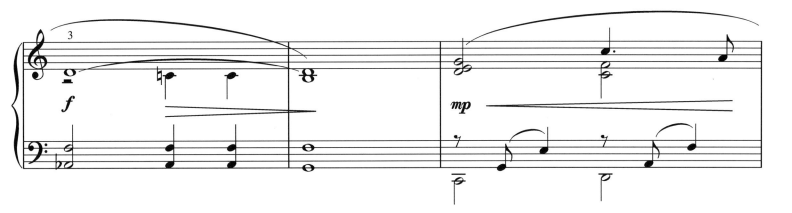

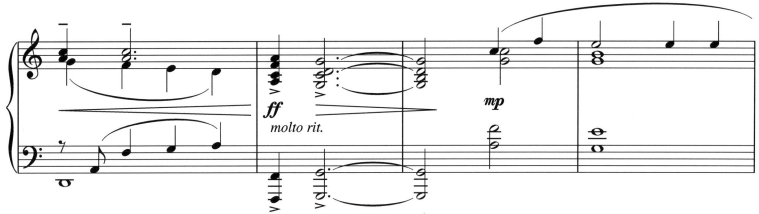

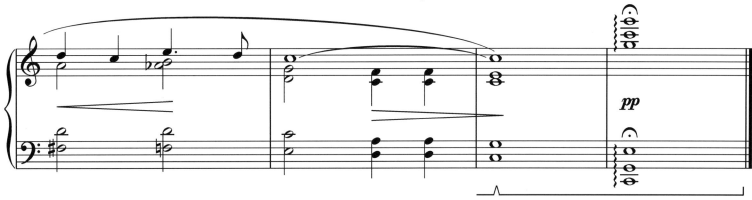

All Hail the Power of Jesus' Name

1. All hail the pow'r of Jesus' name!
   Let angels prostrate fall;
   Bring forth the royal diadem,
   And crown Him Lord of all;
   Bring forth the royal diadem,
   And crown Him Lord of all.

2. Ye chosen seed of Israel's race,
   Ye ransomed from the fall,
   Hail Him who saves you by His grace,
   And crown Him Lord of all.
   Hail Him who saves you by His grace,
   And crown Him Lord of all.

3. Sinners, whose love can ne'er forget
   The wormword and the gall,
   Go spread your trophies at His feet,
   And crown Him Lord of all.
   Go spread your trophies at His feet,
   And crown Him Lord of all.

4. Let ev'ry kindred, ev'ry tribe
   On this terrestrial ball
   To Him all majesty ascribe,
   And crown Him Lord of all.
   To Him all majesty ascribe,
   And crown Him Lord of all.

5. Crown Him, ye martyrs of your God,
   Who from His altar call,
   Extol the Stem of Jesse's Rod,
   And crown Him Lord of all.
   Extol the Stem of Jesse's Rod,
   And crown Him Lord of all.

6. Oh that with yonder sacred throng
   We at His feet may fall.
   We'll join the everlasting song
   And crown Him Lord of all.
   We'll join the everlasting song
   And crown Him Lord of all.

Breathe on Me, Breath of God

1. Breathe on me, Breath of God,
   Fill me with life anew,
   That I may love what Thou dost love,
   And do what Thou wouldst do.

2. Breathe on me, Breath of God,
   Until my heart is pure,
   Until with Thee I will one will,
   To do and to endure.

3. Breathe on me, Breath of God,
   Till I am wholly Thine,
   Until this earthly part of me
   Glows with Thy fire divine.

4. Breathe on me, Breath of God,
   So shall I never die,
   But live with Thee the perfect life
   Of Thine eternity.

Come, Thou Almighty King

1. Come, Thou almighty King,
   Help us Thy name to sing, help us to praise:
   Father all glorious, o'er all victorious,
   Come and reign over us, Ancient of Days.

2. Come, Thou incarnate Word,
   Gird on Thy mighty sword, our prayer attend.
   Come and Thy people bless, and give Thy word success,
   Spirit of holiness, on us descend!

3. Come, holy Comforter,
   Thy sacred witness bear in this glad hour.
   Thou, who almighty art, now rule in ev'ry heart,
   And ne'er from us depart, Spirit of pow'r.

4. To Thee, great One in Three,
   Eternal praises be hence evermore!
   Thy sov'reign majesty may we in glory see,
   And to eternity love and adore!

Come, Thou Fount of Every Blessing

1. Come, Thou Fount of ev'ry blessing,
   Tune my heart to sing Thy grace;
   Streams of mercy, never ceasing,
   Call for songs of loudest praise.
   Teach me some melodious sonnet,
   Sung by flaming tongues above;
   Praise His name, I'm fixed upon it,
   Name of God's redeeming love.

2. Here I raise mine Ebenezer;
   Hither by Thy help I'm come;
   And I hope, by Thy good pleasure,
   Safely to arrive at home.
   Jesus sought me when a stranger,
   Wand'ring from the fold of God;
   He, to rescue me from danger,
   Bought me with His precious blood.

3. O to grace how great a debtor
   Daily I'm constrained to be!
   Let Thy goodness, like a fetter,
   Bind my wand'ring heart to Thee.
   Prone to wander, Lord, I feel it,
   Prone to leave the God I love;
   Here's my heart, O take and seal it,
   Seal it for Thy courts above.

Crown Him with Many Crowns

1. Crown Him with many crowns,
   The Lamb upon His throne.
   Hark! How the heav'nly anthem drowns
   All music but its own.
   Awake, my soul, and sing
   Of Him who died for thee,
   And hail Him as thy matchless King
   Through all eternity.

2. Crown Him the Son of God
   Before the worlds began,
   And ye, who tread where He hath trod,
   Crown Him the Son of Man,
   Who ev'ry grief hath known
   That wrings the human breast,
   And takes and bears them for His own,
   That all in Him may rest.

3. Crown Him the Lord of life,
   Who triumphed o'er the grave,
   Who rose victorious in the strife
   For those He came to save.
   His glories now we sing
   Who died, and rose on high,
   Who died, eternal life to bring,
   And lives that death may die.

4. Crown Him of lords the Lord,
   Who over all doth reign,
   Who once on earth, the incarnate Word,
   For ransomed sinners slain,
   Now lives in realms of light,
   Where saints with angels sing
   Their songs before Him day and night,
   Their God, Redeemer, King.

5. Crown Him the Lord of heav'n,
   Enthroned in worlds above.
   Crown Him the King, to whom is giv'n,
   The wondrous name of Love.
   Crown Him with many crowns,
   As thrones before Him fall.
   Crown Him, ye kings, with many crowns,
   For He is King of all.

God the Omnipotent!

1. God the Omnipotent! King Who ordainest
   Thunder Thy clarion, lightning Thy sword;
   Show forth Thy pity on high where Thou reignest,
   Give to us peace in our time, O Lord.

2. God the All-merciful! Earth hath forsaken
   Thy ways of blessedness, slighted Thy Word;
   Bid not Thy wrath in its terrors awaken;
   Give to us peace in our time, O Lord.

3. God the All-righteous One! Man hath defied Thee;
   Yet to eternity standeth Thy Word,
   Falsehood and wrong shall not tarry beside Thee;
   Give to us peace in our time, O Lord.

4. God the All-wise! By the fire of Thy chast'ning,
   Earth shall to freedom and truth be restored;
   Through the thick darkness Thy kingdom is hast'ning;
   Thou wilt give peace in Thy time, O Lord.

5. So shall Thy children, with thankful devotion,
   Praise Him who saved them from peril and sword,
   Singing in chorus from ocean to ocean,
   Peace to the nations, and praise to the Lord.

God Will Take Care of You

1. Be not dismayed whate'er betide;
   God will take care of you.
   Beneath His wings of love abide;
   God will take care of you.
   Refrain:
   God will take care of you,
   Through every day, o'er all the way.
   He will take care of you;
   God will take care of you.

2. Through days of toil when heart doth fail;
   God will take care of you.
   When dangers fierce your path assail;
   God will take care of you.
   Refrain

3. All you may need He will provide;
   God will take care of you;
   Nothing you ask will be denied;
   God will take care of you.
   Refrain

4. No matter what may be the test,
   God will take care of you.
   Lean, weary one, upon His breast;
   God will take care of you.
   Refrain

I Love to Tell the Story

1. I love to tell the story of unseen things above,
   Of Jesus and His glory, of Jesus and His love.
   I love to tell the story, because I know 'tis true;
   It satisfies my longings as nothing else can do.
   Refrain:
   I love to tell the story, 'twill be my theme in glory,
   To tell the old, old story of Jesus and His love.

2. I love to tell the story, more wonderful it seems
   Than all the golden fancies of all our golden dreams.
   I love to tell the story, it did so much for me;
   And that is just the reason I tell it now to thee.
   Refrain

3. I love to tell the story; 'tis pleasant to repeat
   What seems, each time I tell it, more wonderfully sweet.
   I love to tell the story, for some have never heard
   The message of salvation from God's own holy Word.
   Refrain

4. I love to tell the story, for those who know it best
   Seem hungering and thirsting to hear it like the rest.
   And when, in scenes of glory, I sing the new, new song,
   'Twill be the old, old story that I have loved so long.
   Refrain

I Surrender All

1. All to Jesus I surrender,
   All to Him I freely give;
   I will ever love and trust Him,
   In His presence daily live.
   Refrain:
   I surrender all, I surrender all,
   All to Thee, my blessed Savior,
   I surrender all.

2. All to Jesus I surrender,
   Humbly at His feet I bow;
   Worldly pleasures all forsaken,
   Take me, Jesus, take me now.
   Refrain

3. All to Jesus I surrender,
   Make me, Savior, wholly Thine;
   Let me feel the Holy Spirit,
   Truly know that Thou art mine.
   Refrain

4. All to Jesus I surrender,
   Lord, I give myself to Thee;
   Fill me with Thy love and power,
   Let Thy blessing fall on me.
   Refrain

5. All to Jesus I surrender,
   Now I feel the sacred flame;
   O the joy of full salvation!
   Glory, glory, to His Name!
   Refrain

I've Got Peace Like a River

1. I've got peace like a river,
   I've got peace like a river,
   I've got peace like a river in my soul.
   I've got peace like a river,
   I've got peace like a river,
   I've got peace like a river in my soul.

2. I've got love like an ocean,
   I've got love like an ocean,
   I've got love like an ocean in my soul.
   I've got love like an ocean,
   I've got love like an ocean,
   I've got love like an ocean in my soul.

3. I've got joy like a fountain,
   I've got joy like a fountain,
   I've got joy like a fountain in my soul.
   I've got joy like a fountain,
   I've got joy like a fountain,
   I've got joy like a fountain in my soul.

Immortal, Invisible

1. Immortal, invisible, God only wise,
   In light inaccessible hid from our eyes,
   Most blessed, most glorious, the Ancient of Days,
   Almighty, victorious, Thy great name we praise.

2. Unresting, unhasting, and silent as light,
   Nor wanting, nor wasting, Thou rulest in might;
   Thy justice like mountains high soaring above
   Thy clouds, which are fountains of goodness and love.

3. To all, life Thou givest, to both great and small;
   In all life Thou livest, the true life of all;
   We blossom and flourish like leaves on the tree,
   And wither and perish; but naught changeth Thee.

4. Thou reignest in glory, Thou rulest in light,
   Thine angels adore Thee, all veiling their sight;
   All praise we would render; oh help us to see
   'Tis only the splendor of light hideth Thee!

O Worship the King

1. O worship the King, all glorious above,
   O gratefully sing His pow'r and His love;
   Our Shield and Defender, the Ancient of Days,
   Pavilioned in splendor, and girded with praise.

2. O tell of His might, O sing of His grace,
   Whose robe is the light, whose canopy space!
   His chariots of wrath the deep thunderclouds form,
   And dark is His path on the wings of the storm.

3. Thy bountiful care what tongue can recite?
   It breathes in the air, it shines in the light;
   It streams from the hills, it descends to the plain,
   And sweetly distills in the dew and the rain.

4. Frail children of dust, and feeble as frail,
   In Thee do we trust, nor find Thee to fail;
   Thy mercies how tender, how firm to the end,
   Our Maker, Defender, Redeemer and Friend.

Praise to the Lord, The Almighty

1. Praise to the Lord, the Almighty, the King of creation!
   O my soul, praise Him, for He is thy health
      and salvation!
   All ye who hear, now to His temple draw near;
   Join me in glad adoration!

2. Praise to the Lord, who o'er all things
      so wondrously reigneth,
   Shelters thee under His wings, yes,
      so gently sustaineth!
   Hast thou not seen how all thy longings have been
   Granted in what He ordaineth?

3. Praise to the Lord, who doth prosper thy
      work and defend thee;
   Surely His goodness and mercy here daily attend thee.
   Ponder anew what the Almighty can do,
   If with His love He befriend thee.

4. Praise to the Lord! O let all that is in me adore Him!
   All that hath life and breath, come now
      with praises before Him.
   Let the Amen sound from His people again:
   Gladly for aye we adore Him.

Softly and Tenderly

1. Softly and tenderly Jesus is calling,
   Calling for you and for me;
   See, on the portals He's waiting and watching,
   Watching for you and for me.
   Refrain:
   Come home, come home,
   Ye who are weary, come home;
   Earnestly, tenderly, Jesus is calling,
   Calling, O sinner, come home!

2. Why should we tarry when Jesus is pleading,
   Pleading for you and for me?
   Why should we linger and heed not His mercies,
   Mercies for you and for me?
   Refrain

3. Time is now fleeting, the moments are passing,
   Passing from you and from me;
   Shadows are gathering, death's night is coming,
   Coming for you and for me.
   Refrain

4. O, for the wonderful love He has promised,
   Promised for you and for me!
   Though we have sinned, He has mercy and pardon,
   Pardon for you and for me.
   Refrain

This Is My Father's World

1. This is my Father's world, and to my list'ning ears
   All nature sings, and round me rings the music
       of the spheres.
   This is my Father's world: I rest me in the thought
   Of rocks and trees, of skies and seas
   His hand the wonders wrought.

2. This is my Father's world, the birds their carols raise,
   The morning light, the lily white, declare their
       Maker's praise.
   This is my Father's world: He shines in all that's fair;
   In the rustling grass I hear Him pass,
   He speaks to me ev'rywhere.

3. This is my Father's world, O let me ne'er forget
   That though the wrong seems oft so strong,
       God is the Ruler yet.
   This is my Father's world: The battle is not done;
   Jesus who died shall be satisfied,
   And earth and heav'n be one.

'Tis So Sweet to Trust in Jesus

1. 'Tis so sweet to trust in Jesus,
   Just to take Him at His Word,
   Just to rest upon His promise,
   Just to know, "Thus says the Lord."
   Refrain:
   Jesus, Jesus, how I trust Him!
   How I've proved Him o'er and o'er
   Jesus, Jesus, precious Jesus!
   O for grace to trust Him more!

2. O how sweet to trust in Jesus,
   Just to trust His cleansing blood,
   Just in simple faith to plunge me
   'Neath the healing, cleansing flood!
   Refrain

3. Yes, 'tis sweet to trust in Jesus,
   Just from sin and self to cease,
   Just from Jesus simply taking
   Life and rest, and joy and peace.
   Refrain

4. I'm so glad I learned to trust Thee,
   Precious Jesus, Savior, Friend;
   And I know that Thou art with me,
   Wilt be with me to the end.
   Refrain

Were You There?

1. Were you there when they crucified my Lord?
    Were you there when they crucified my Lord?
    Oh! Sometimes it causes me to tremble, tremble, tremble.
    Were you there when they crucified my Lord?

2. Were you there when they nailed Him to the tree?
    Were you there when they nailed Him to the tree?
    Oh! Sometimes it causes me to tremble, tremble, tremble.
    Were you there when they nailed Him to the tree?

3. Were you there when they laid Him in the tomb?
    Were you there when they laid Him in the tomb?
    Oh! Sometimes it causes me to tremble, tremble, tremble.
    Were you there when they laid Him in the tomb?

4. Were you there when He rose up from the dead?
    Were you there when He rose up from the dead?
    Oh! Sometimes I feel like shouting glory, glory, glory!
    Were you there when He rose up from the dead?